KRISHNA
AN INVISIBLE FRIEND

by

Nishita Chaitanya

Illustrations by: Rohan Khedekar

C·H·I·N·M·A·Y·A   B·A·L·A   K·A·T·H·A

In a small village on a hill near the forest was a small house. A kind gentle lady and her sweet little son lived there alone. They missed the father who had passed on a few years before. They were happy to have each other, and happy to have the small house.

They were very poor. They had little food to eat, just a few clothes to wear, and there were hardly any toys for the little boy to play with.

Their village was small and did not have a school. But the gentle lady wanted her sweet son to go to school. She wanted him to learn and to be clever and bright.

Through the forest, down the slopes, around the corner, in the next village, there was a school.

There were classrooms with teachers. There were books and ballpens, chalkboards and computers. There were playgrounds - and lots of children!

"Oh, how I wish my son could go there!" the gentle lady thought. So she sent the little boy to the school on the other side, through the forest, down the slopes, around the corner, in the next village.

But her son was very little and the school was very far away. Very very far away indeed. Also, going through the forest was scary.

The trees seemed so tall, the creatures made such strange noises, and it was quite dark in the thickest parts of the forest. So the little boy did not like walking to school.

He liked the school. He liked the teachers and the other children. He liked the subjects and the games. He even liked the homework. But he did not like walking through the dark scary forest.

He would wake up in the morning and say to his mother, "I don't want to go, Mama. Can I stay home with you today, please?"

"But how will you learn if you stay home with me?" his mother would answer as she packed his lunch.

One day as he was walking back home through the forest, he was more scared than ever. He thought something was following him. Pushing and panting, he ran as fast as his little legs could carry him. But he tripped and fell and bruised his knees. Eventually he reached home crying.

"I hate the forest! I hate school! I hate everything!" he said to his mother. "I am never going back!"

His mother was sad. She was sad because her little boy was scared and crying. She was sad because her little boy was all alone. She was sad because they did not have much money and she had to work, so she could not take him to school herself.

Who could help her?

She knew she was not alone. She was never alone.

Krishna was always with her.

Krishna always listened to her. Krishna always helped her. And so she prayed.

Krishna has many names. One of his names is Gopal, and this is the name the gentle lady liked best.

She bent down towards her son She held his sweet dear face in her hands and gently wiped away his tears.

In a soft, encouraging voice she said, "My dear child, you are not alone. I shall tell you a secret."

"A secret?" The little boy's eyes became wide, and he moved closer to his mother as he asked, "What secret, Mama?"

"There is someone looking after you in the forest," his mother replied, almost in a whisper. "You have an older brother. He stays in the forest, and he protects you whenever you need him."

"Really, Mama? Do I really have a brother in the forest? What does he do there? Why does he not come home to be with us?" the puzzled boy asked.

"My dear, your brother looks after the calves in the forest, that's why he does not come home. But don't worry, he will come to you.

"Whenever you are in the forest and you get scared, just call out to him with all your heart, 'Gopal Bhaiya! Gopal Bhaiya!' And he will come to you. He will surely come to you."

"Gopal Bhaiya?" said the little boy.

"Gopal is his name and Bhaiya means 'brother'. He is older than you so you have to call him 'Bhaiya'," explained the gentle mother.

The little boy was delighted he had a brother. He was so excited to meet his older brother. He was glad he was not alone.

The next morning he woke up early. After breakfast, he ran to the forest. He yelled, "Gopal Bhaiya, Gopal Bhaiya" and looked around. "Where are you, Gopal Bhaiya?" he called again, and looked around once more.

But nobody came.

The dark scary forest was quiet. The large shadows of the trees swayed back and forth with the wind. The little boy was afraid. He was very afraid.

Remembering what his mother had told him, with all his heart, he cried out loud, "Gopal Bhaiya, Gopal Bhaiya, PLEASE HELP ME! Please come out and help me, I'm scared." And the sweet little boy burst into tears.

From behind a tree, out popped a little head. With a giggle.

This lovely bubbly blue boy had thick curly black hair and big bright brown eyes, with a naughty, naughty smile. And there was a beautiful peacock feather on the side of his head.

He looked a little older and taller than the frightened boy.

"Gopal Bhaiya? Is that you?" the little one whispered because he couldn't believe what he was seeing.

Krishna came out from behind the tree and put an arm around the little boy's shoulders.

The little boy looked up into Krishna's eyes. He felt so safe, so unafraid, and loved. It felt like magic, magic that makes us happy.

"I heard your call so I came running," said Krishna, encouragingly. "Why are you crying?

You never have to cry. I'm right here for you whenever you need me."

The little boy wiped away his tears. He smiled, he giggled, and then he chuckled. He was happy. He was thrilled. He was ecstatic. He had a brother, a truly wonderful brother.

"Gopal Bhaiya, why don't you come home? Why haven't you come before? Why do you stay only in the forest?" The little boy started asking many questions, like most little boys do.

Krishna answered all the questions as they walked through the forest till they got to the other side. Krishna hugged the little boy and said, "Little one, I'll be right here for you. I'll always be with you whenever you need me."

The little boy was sure he would see his brother again. So off he went down the slopes, around the corner and into his school.

But the moment school was over, he quickly ran up the slopes towards the forest. "Gopal Bhaiya," he called out, "can you hear me?"

Out popped the cute little head again.

"Catch me if you can," bubbly blue Krishna yelled back as he started running through the forest.

Now every day before and after school the little boy would meet his Gopal Bhaiya in the forest. Along the way Krishna would show the little boy all sorts of wonderful creatures that lived in the forest.

He showed the little boy the cheery chirping birds and the buzzing-wuzzing insects. Flitter flutter here and there, here and there, they flew all day long.

Then Krishna showed him the busy bushy-tailed squirrels. Up and down, up and down, up and down the branches they went. Then there were the funny-looking moustachioed monkeys that swung from tree to tree.

Krishna also showed him so many different flowers in so many different shapes and sizes, and they all smelled so nice, each one different from the other!

The forest was no longer scary, it was fascinating.

The little boy was no longer afraid, he was joyful.

The little boy knew that he was never alone. Gopal Bhaiya was always with him.

He had a friend, he had a brother, he had a guide.

School was coming to an end. Soon there would be holidays. Every year on the last day of school, all the little boys and girls would bring something for their teacher. Some would bring food, some would bring presents and some would bring money.

The little boy wanted to take something to school too. But what? He did not have much food. He felt terrible that all the other children would have gifts to offer while he had nothing.

But then he had an idea!

The next day in the forest he asked Krishna, "Gopal Bhaiya, can you give me something to take to school for my teacher, please?"

"Of course I can," said Krishna. "I shall have it ready for you tomorrow, on your way to school."

The next day as the little boy came running up the slope he saw Krishna holding a small pot. It had some ice-cream inside it. And it was crunchy-munchy flavoured!

When the little boy got to school, he saw that all the other children had brought big and beautiful gifts for the teacher.

There were baskets of fruit, pouches of nuts and jars of jam. There were also bags of chocolates, cookies and candies, all tied with ribbons.

The boy felt ashamed. Everybody else's gift was so big and fancy, and he had just a super small pot of ice-cream. He did not want to give it to his teacher after all. He stood in one corner of the room where nobody would notice him.

But his teacher saw him looking sad. He was a good, caring teacher, and wanted everyone to feel nice in his class. So he called out to the little boy, "What are you hiding there? I know you brought me something very special," said the teacher, encouragingly.

The little boy took out the tiny pot and showed it to his teacher. The other children laughed at the inni-mini gift.

The boy looked down and his face turned red with embarrassment. But the teacher looked at the little boy and said, "Thank you, little boy, I love your gift."

The teacher took the tiny pot and emptied it out into a big tub. He was just about to return the pot to the little boy when, suddenly, he noticed:

Instead of being empty, the tiny pot was FULL!

The teacher poured the ice-cream out again and turned the pot back up - it was full again!

The teacher was surprised. The little boy was surprised. All the other little boys and girls could not believe their eyes either. Everyone was surprised, and they all gathered around the tiny pot to see what was happening.

The teacher emptied out the pot again. He did this one more time, and again, and again... . But the pot would not get empty, it was always full!

What a wonderful gift this was indeed!

The children screamed out in joy, "What magic! What fun!"

The teacher smiled in wonderment, "How strange! How nice!"

The little boy laughed in delight, "How perfect! So cool!"

"Where did you get such a pot?" asked the puzzled teacher of the bright-eyed little boy. "My brother gave it to me," answered the child, who was now beaming, proud of his gift AND his brother.

"Your brother? I did not know you have a brother. Who is your brother?" asked the teacher, even more puzzled.

"Gopal Bhaiya. He takes care of the calves in the forest. He is the most handsome and strongest boy, with a peacock feather in his curly black hair, with big brown eyes, and a naughty smile."

As the little boy talked about his brother, the teacher understood that this was Lord Krishna.

The teacher wanted to meet this brother. The other children also wanted to meet this great brother. Everyone wanted to meet the little boy's brother.

So all of them went to the forest. The little boy stood at the edge of the forest and called out, "Gopal Bhaiya, where are you? Please come out."

They all waited. But Krishna did not come.

Again he yelled, "Gopal Bhaiya, please come out. I have brought my friends and my teacher. They all want to see you." And they waited, but Krishna did not appear.

Again and again he called out but Krishna did not come. They waited and waited and waited, but Krishna did not turn up.

Confused, the little boy cried, "Gopal Bhaiya, why aren't you coming out? Are you angry with me? Please come out just this once."

They all waited. But Krishna still did not come.

The earnest teacher closed his eyes, filled himself with love. He thought of Krishna and called out from his heart.

The other little boys and girls also closed their eyes, and filled themselves with love. They saw Krishna in their minds and with devotion called, "Gopal Bhaiya".

They believed. They really truly believed: "Gopal Bhaiya will come. He will surely come."

From behind a tree, out popped a little head. He smiled. He giggled. He chuckled.

This lovely bubbly blue boy had thick curly black hair and big bright brown eyes, with a naughty, naughty smile.

It was MAGIC !

Everyone was happy. Everyone was thrilled. Everyone was ecstatic.

They had **SEEN** Krishna.

Have you seen Krishna?

Do you know the magic?

You do, don't you?

Close your eyes, fill yourself with love, and believe. With all your heart call out to him, "Gopal Bhaiya!"

If you do, you will **SEE** him too!